EVERYDAY STEM

MOMENTUM

Christopher Forest and John Willis

AV2

www.av2books.com

Step 1
Go to **www.av2books.com**

Step 2
Enter this unique code
CKIEQ3UFG

Step 3
Explore your interactive eBook!

AV2 is optimized for use on any device

Your interactive eBook comes with...

Contents
Browse a live contents page to easily navigate through resources

Audio
Listen to sections of the book read aloud

Videos
Watch informative video clips

Weblinks
Gain additional information for research

Try This!
Complete activities and hands-on experiments

Key Words
Study vocabulary, and complete a matching word activity

Quizzes
Test your knowledge

Slideshows
View images and captions

... and much, much more!

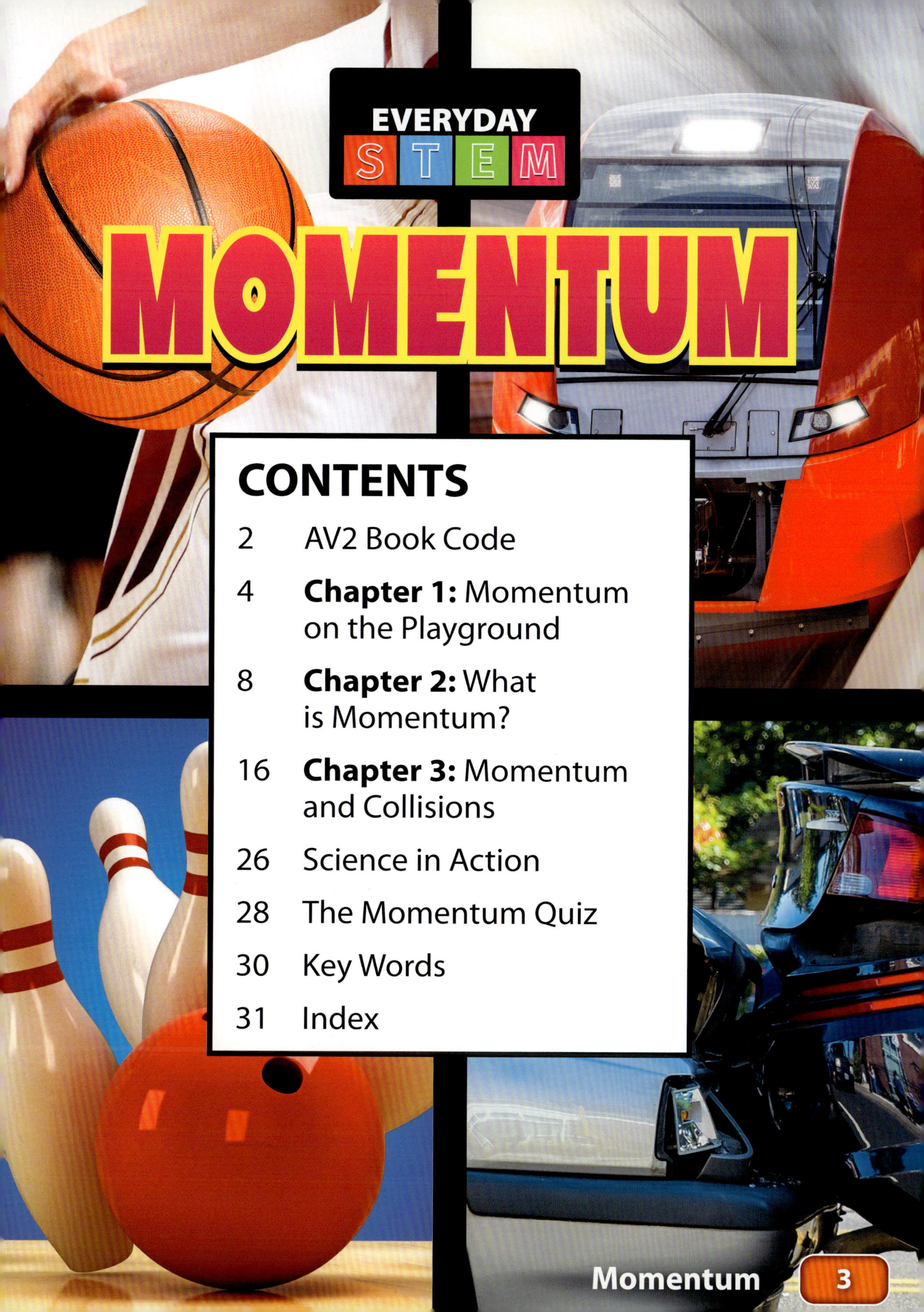

MOMENTUM

CONTENTS

CHAPTER ONE

Momentum on the Playground

Andre is at the playground. He climbs the stairs to the top of the slide. Then, he stands and waits until it is his turn to go down. While Andre is waiting, he is at rest. This means he is not moving.

Finally, it is Andre's turn. He goes down the slide. His body is in **motion**. He goes faster as he moves down the slide.

Momentum is a measurement that tells people about an object's motion. Any object that is moving has momentum. On the playground, Andre was moving while he was going down the slide. For this reason, Andre had momentum.

Other playground activities, such as swinging, also involve momentum.

CHAPTER TWO

What Is Momentum?

Two things determine an object's momentum. One of these is the object's **velocity**. This describes both the speed of the object and the direction it is moving. For example, think of a large truck.

Cars that are not moving have no momentum.

On the highway, the truck usually has a high speed. The same truck driving in a parking lot usually has a low speed. The truck has more momentum when it is moving quickly. It has less momentum when it is moving slowly. If the truck is not moving, it has no momentum.

The other thing that affects an object's momentum is its **mass**. Mass is related to the amount and type of material in an object.

Imagine that a car and a skateboard are rolling down the street. Suppose they are moving at the same speed. The car has more mass. For this reason, the car has more momentum. The skateboard has less mass. That means the skateboard has less momentum.

Momentum affects how difficult it is to stop a moving object. For example, a slow-rolling soccer ball has low speed and low mass. A person can easily stop the ball because it does not have much momentum. A fast-moving train has high speed and high mass. It is much harder to stop because it has a lot of momentum.

Trains need a large amount of space in order to slow to a stop.

A hockey puck loses momentum because of friction between the puck and the ice.

A moving object keeps its momentum unless a force causes it to change. Sometimes an object is slowed down by the surface it moves across. This can happen because of friction.

Think of a hockey puck sliding across ice. There is **friction** between the puck and the ice. This friction causes the puck to lose momentum. In time, the puck will come to a stop.

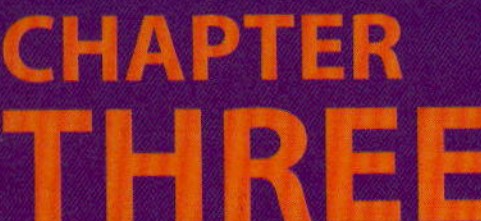

Momentum and Collisions

Sometimes one object bumps into a second object. This is called a **collision**. During the collision, the two objects **exert** forces on each other. This causes the momentum of each object to change.

When cars collide, they exchange momentum. This often causes damage to the cars.

If no other forces are acting on the objects, the total momentum stays the same. This means both objects experience the same change in momentum but in **opposite** directions.

For example, think of two objects colliding along a line. Imagine that the first object is in motion. The second object is at rest. Suppose the two objects have the same mass. In this case, the first object will stop. It will give all of its momentum to the second object.

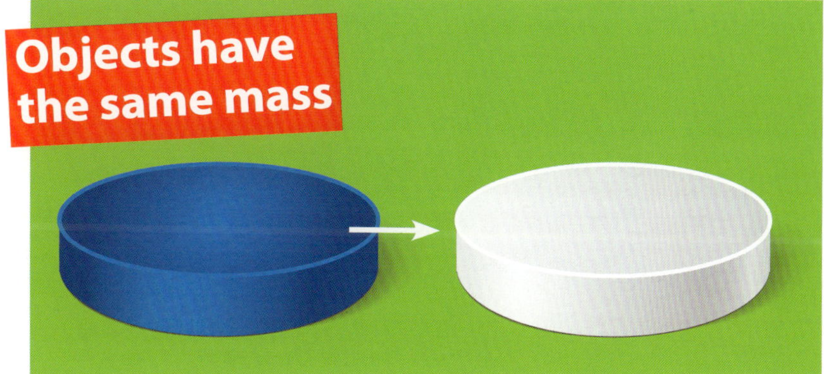

Now suppose the first object is lighter than the second object. In this case, the first object will bounce backward because of the collision. The second object will move forward.

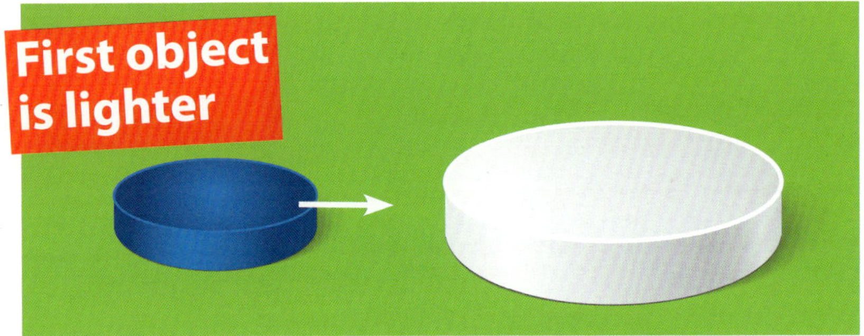

Finally, suppose the first object is heavier than the second. Again, the second object will move forward. But the first object will keep moving forward, too. It will just be slower. In all three examples, the total momentum stays the same if no other forces are acting on the objects.

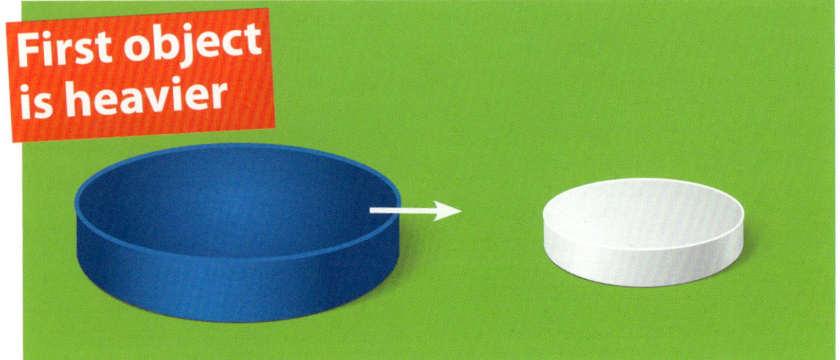

HOW COLLISIONS AFFECT MOMENTUM

Before	After
 Both objects have the same mass.	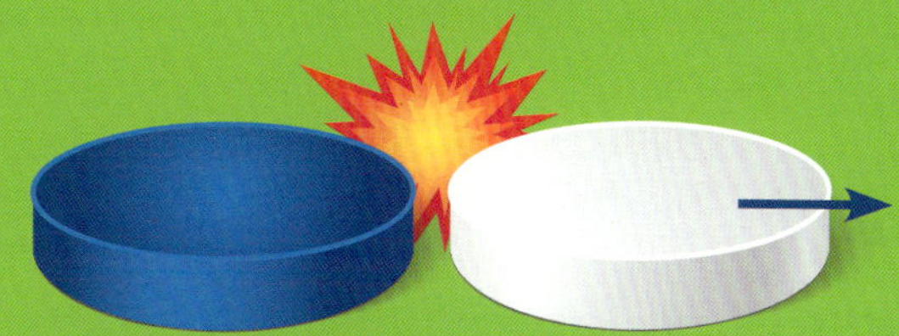 The first object stops. The second object moves forward.
 The first object is lighter.	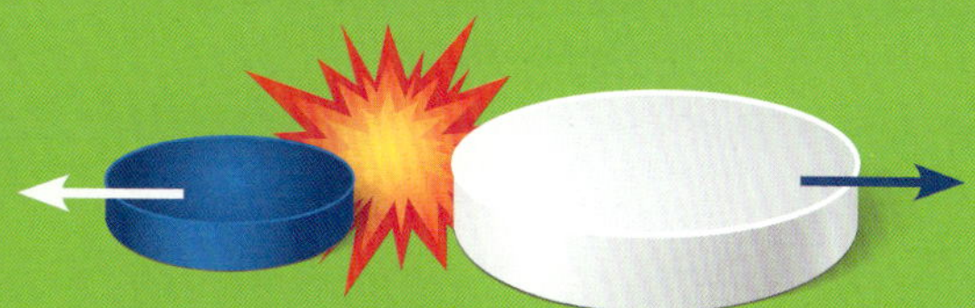 The first object bounces back. The second object moves forward.
 The first object is heavier.	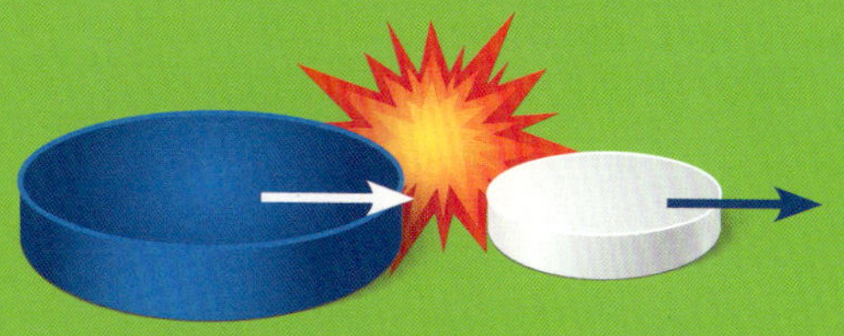 Both objects move forward.

Momentum is important in many activities that people enjoy. For example, all sports involve people or objects moving. That means all sports involve momentum.

Hitting a baseball causes the ball's momentum to change. The ball's mass does not change. But after the ball is hit, it leaves the bat in a different direction. If the speed or direction of the ball changes, the momentum changes.

A ball's momentum
changes after it is hit.

Like all sports, basketball involves momentum.

In football, a large player running fast has lots of momentum. A small player running slowly has much less momentum. This is why it is harder to tackle the large player running fast. That player has more momentum, so it is harder to get that player to stop.

Momentum is an important part of our lives. Anytime you are moving, think about momentum!

Science in Action

Momentum with Scooter Boards

How does momentum depend on mass and velocity? Do this experiment to find out.

Get two identical scooter boards. Also, gather a group of friends.

Choose two friends with approximately the same weight. Have them sit on the scooters near each other.

STEP 3

One friend should use his or her feet to push the scooters apart. Do the two scooters move away at about the same speed? Or is one moving faster than the other? Does it matter which friend does the pushing?

STEP 4

Now repeat this experiment with different friends. A heavier friend should be on one scooter. A lighter friend should be on the other. Do the two scooters move away at about the same speed? Or is one moving faster than the other? If they have different speeds, which friend is moving the fastest?

THE MOMENTUM QUIZ

- 1 -

Does an object that is not moving have momentum?

A. No

- 2 -

What two things determine an object's momentum?

A. Velocity and mass

- 4 -

Are mass and momentum the same thing?

A. No

- 3 -

Why is it hard to stop a fast-moving train?

A. Because it has a lot of momentum

- 5 -

Is friction a force?

A. Yes

- 6 -

What is a collision?

A. When one object bumps into another

- 7 -

Do collisions affect momentum?

A. Yes

- 8 -

Will a moving object stop moving if no other force acts on it?

A. No

- 9 -

What does velocity describe?

A. The speed and direction of an object

- 10 -

Can friction stop an object with momentum?

A. Yes

Key Words

collision: when two objects come in contact

exert: to apply or make use of

friction: a force that happens when two objects rub against each other

mass: the amount of matter in an object

motion: movement

opposite: different or reverse

velocity: the speed of an object and the direction it moves in

Index

Get the best of both worlds.

AV2 bridges the gap between print and digital.

The expandable resources toolbar enables quick access to content including **videos**, **audio**, **activities**, **weblinks**, **slideshows**, **quizzes**, and **key words**.

Animated videos make static images come alive.

Resource icons on each page help readers to further **explore key concepts**.

Published by AV2
14 Penn Plaza, 9th Floor New York, NY 10122
Website: www.av2books.com

Library of Congress Control Number: 2020936968

ISBN 978-1-7911-2388-8 (hardcover)
ISBN 978-1-7911-2389-5 (softcover)
ISBN 978-1-7911-2390-1 (multi-user eBook)
ISBN 978-1-7911-2391-8 (single-user eBook)

Printed in Guangzhou, China
1 2 3 4 5 6 7 8 9 0 24 23 22 21 20

052020
101319

Designer: Terry Paulhus Project Coordinator: Priyanka Das

Every reasonable effort has been made to trace ownership and to obtain permission to reprint copyright material. The publisher would be pleased to have any errors or omissions brought to its attention so that they may be corrected in subsequent printings.

The publisher acknowledges Getty Images, iStock, and Shutterstock as its primary image suppliers for this title.

First published by Focus Readers in 2018.